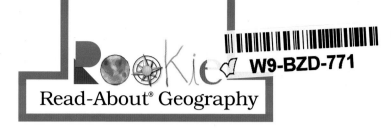

Read-About® Geography

W9-BZD-771

North America

By Allan Fowler

Consultant
Linda Cornwell
Coordinator of School Quality and Professional Improvement
Indiana State Teachers Association

Property of
Lisa Efthymiou

Children's Press®
A Division of Grolier Publishing
New York London Hong Kong Sydney
Danbury, Connecticut

Designer: Herman Adler Design Group
Photo Researcher: Caroline Anderson
The photo on the cover shows a view of Rocky Mountain National Park
in Colorado.

Library of Congress Cataloging-in-Publication Data

Fowler, Allan.
    North America / by Allan Fowler.
        p. cm. — (Rookie read-about geography)
    Includes index.
    Summary: A simple introduction to the geographic features, people, and
animals of the continent of North America.
        ISBN 0-516-21671-6 (lib. bdg.)   0-516-27299-3 (pbk.)
        1. North America—Juvenile literature. 2. North America—
Geography—Juvenile literature. [1. North America.] I. Title. II. Series.
    E38.5.F69   2001
    970—dc21
                                                    00-027560

The biggest pieces of land on Earth are called continents.

There are seven continents.

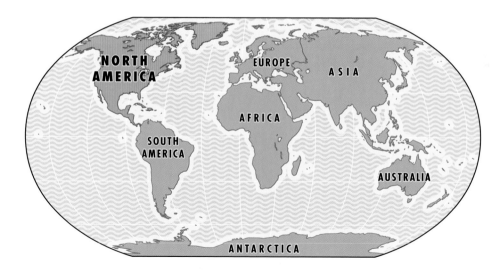

You can find North America on a globe. It is a big, wide continent.

North America covers more than three thousand miles between the Atlantic and Pacific (pa-SIF-ik) oceans.

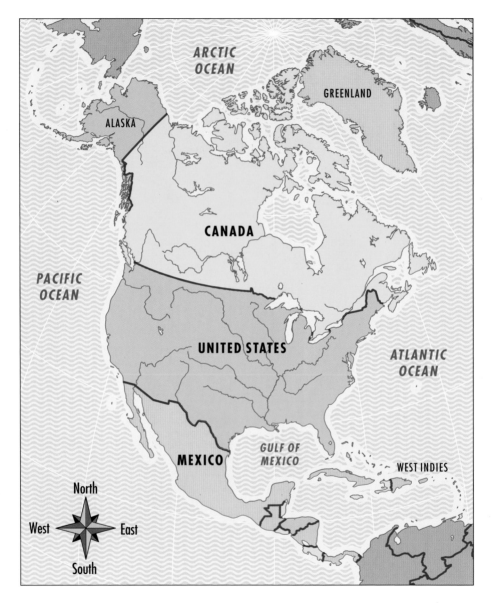

ARCTIC OCEAN

GREENLAND

ALASKA

CANADA

PACIFIC OCEAN

UNITED STATES

ATLANTIC OCEAN

MEXICO

GULF OF MEXICO

WEST INDIES

North

West

East

South

The United States and
Canada make up the wide
part of the continent. Mexico
is at the narrow bottom.

Greenland is at the top
of North America. It is
the world's largest island.

The islands of the
West Indies (IN-dees)
are also often included
in North America.

The Rocky Mountains cross the western parts of North America. They stretch across Canada and the United States.

Their tall peaks, or tops, are rocky and bare.

The Appalachian
(ap-uh-LAY-chee-an)
Mountains cross the
eastern parts of North
America. They are
not as tall as the
Rocky Mountains.

The Appalachian
Mountains are covered
with trees.

Wheat field

Most of the land between the western and eastern mountains is flat.

In the United States, farmers grow wheat and corn on these flat lands called the Great Plains.

Cornfield

The Missouri (mi-ZUR-ee) River and the Ohio River cross the plains. They join the Mississippi River. The Mississippi is the mightiest river of them all.

Mississippi River

Some parts of North America can be very cold. The state of Alaska, most of northern Canada, and Greenland are often covered in snow.

Alaska

Canada

Greenland

Other parts of North America are warm almost all year, such as Florida, Mexico, and the islands of the West Indies.

Many people travel to these places to enjoy the ocean beaches.

Most of North America
is temperate.

That means the weather
changes with the seasons.

Some parts of North America are very dry.

In California's Mojave (mo-HAV-ee) Desert, it is too dry for most plants to grow.

Other parts of North America are very wet.

Alligators swim in Florida's swampy Everglades.

Visitors come to North America from all over the world. Some come to see the Grand Canyon in Arizona.

Others stop at the amazing
waterfalls of Niagara
(ny–AG–a–ra) Falls.

Many visitors travel to
the Statue of Liberty
in New York Harbor.

She has welcomed
many people to North
America for more than
one hundred years!

Words You Know

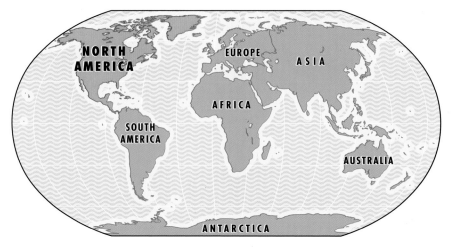

continents

Appalachian Mountains

Everglades

globe

Grand Canyon

Mojave Desert

Niagara Falls

Rocky Mountains

Statue of Liberty

31

Index

About the Author

Allan Fowler is a freelance writer with a background in advertising. Born in New York, he now lives in Chicago and enjoys traveling.

Photo Credits

Photographs ©: Mary Liz Austin: 20; Nance S. Trueworthy: 5, 31 top left; New England Stock Photo: 11, 30 left (Bill Lea); Peter Arnold Inc.: 17 bottom (IFA), 9, 31 bottom left (Art Twomey), 25, 30 right (Richard Weiss); Stone: 15, 26, 31 top right (Tom Bean), 21 (Terry Donnelly), 22, 31 center left (Jack Dykinga), 18 (Bruce Hands), 16 (R.G.K. Photography), 12 (Andy Sacks), 29, 31 bottom right (A & L Sinibaldi); Terry Donnelly: cover, 13; Wolfgang Käehler: 17, 27, 31 center right.

Maps by Bob Italiano.